You Celebrate... You!

What Do You Do
When You Find Out
Your Husband Is Gay?

You Celebrate... You!

Carolyn M. Brown

iUniverse, Inc.
Bloomington

You... Celebrate You!
What Do You Do When You Find Out Your Husband is Gay?

iUniverse books may be ordered through booksellers or by contacting:

iUniverse
1663 Liberty Drive
Bloomington, IN 47403
www.iuniverse.com
1-800-Authors (1-800-288-4677)

ISBN: 978-1-4502-8061-7 (sc)
ISBN: 978-1-4502-8063-1 (dj)
ISBN: 978-1-4502-8062-4 (ebk)

Printed in the United States of America

iUniverse rev. date: 02/16/2011

You ... Celebrate You!

Dedicated in loving memory to my daughter,
Jennifer Lyn Fife,
Forever in our hearts!
November 23, 1974 – June 2, 2010.

During a conversation Jen and I had in her last week in this world, she made a statement about her father and me, saying, "You two are just special in the way you get along."

Contents

Foreword

Each one of us will come to a point in time when we begin to take responsibility for our lives. It is from that moment on that we realize everything we have attracted to us, in some way, paves the road to our highest good. Our past karma, along with our chosen life path, dictates the type of environment best suited for our most rapid growth. We choose, then, not to take the easy way out, but to embrace the path of greatest resistance so that we learn and progress *the most* during our sojourn on earth.

Relationships provide for us some of our greatest lessons. They are the one thing we cannot escape. We attract to us the perfect partners that will take us to our next stage of spiritual development.

In order to truly understand the depth of our relationships, we must acknowledge that, before we arrive in physical form, we make a pact with other souls who will join us on the journey. We say to each other, "Let us meet up in the physical world. Let us treat each other in a certain way so that together we will grow and evolve to a higher level." We make these arrangements prior to incarnating on Earth. The problem is, once we arrive, we forget these contracts exist. As a result, we allow ourselves to get upset with others and with life itself.

We are here on Earth to connect with people, so it is important to make it our business to learn how to interact and grow from one another. In my practice as a Reiki healer and life coach, I have found that one of the most common lessons to be learned in life is how to love unconditionally. That means total acceptance: love without attachment.

You are about to share in the journey of one woman's experience to unconditional acceptance. Carolyn Brown is an enlightened soul who has used her own life path to teach others how to celebrate themselves through adversity. Within the pages of *You... Celebrate You!* Carolyn shares her deepest thoughts and greatest awakenings.

Through the course of this book, and through her seminars and retreats, I believe that Carolyn will be the candle that others will light their candles from. Get ready to have your heart and mind opened; I trust you will.

Many blessings on your journey,

Elisabeth Fayt, international speaker
and author of *Paving It Forward*
www.pavingitforward.com

Preface

After being married for twenty-seven years, I discovered my first husband was gay. Devastated, I looked for answers but found there was very little literature on the subject, and I could find no adequate support available to women facing this situation. Determined to fill the void of information, I wrote the first edition of *You ... Celebrate You!* (2007).

It was gratefully received by women in similar situations, and it soon became apparent that a second version needed to be written— one that included the sharing of feelings and circumstances by the women and families dealing with the dynamics of gay spousal betrayal—hence, this book.

The feelings expressed by way of quotes throughout this version of *You ... Celebrate You!* were received via anonymous e-mails. Therefore, no references are attached, and they have been edited solely to respect the privacy of the contributing individuals. I have not provided their full, in-depth stories; my goal is simply to provide, through the words of others, a sense of support, comfort, and hope to those who find themselves in similar circumstances.

This new version also reflects my ongoing personal growth through continuous study in the areas of the Law of Attraction, meditation, and the teachings of Self Realization Fellowship (SRF), founded by Paramahansa Yogananda. All have contributed in allowing me to approach each and every situation in life with a deeper, richer understanding of what it really is all about. It is my honor to pass these insights and reflections on, in the hopes of encouraging others to seek the wisdom and power within themselves as well, in whatever form they choose.

I would like to take this opportunity to thank Elisabeth Fayt, international speaker and advocate of the Law of Attraction and author of the amazing, life-changing book *Paving It Forward*, for her encouragement and mentoring, and for introducing me to my current husband, John, and to SRF.

I also would like to thank Janet Bray Attwood and Chris Attwood, authors and founders of the world-renowned dynamic self-discovery system, *The Passion Test*, for allowing me to include the Passion test™ within the pages of this book. I am truly honored.

Thanks also to Iyanla Vanzant, author of *Until Today, Daily Devotions for Spiritual Growth and Peace of Mind*, for the strength her devotions have provided me and for her permission to include two wonderful devotions that I hope inspire others.

Also, many thanks to Anna-Mae Sebastian for her work in editing this version.

And to my husband, John, I extend my eternal gratitude for his incredible assistance and support.

It is my sincere wish that this book will encourage all women, especially those going through their stories of pain and deceit, to discover what lies beyond the hurt and the anger—to rediscover themselves and celebrate their lives, their passions, and their joys, and to ultimately understand that everything happens for a reason.

What do you do when you find out your husband is gay?
You ... Celebrate You!

"It matters not what happens to us. What matters is how we respond."

—Elisabeth Fayt

Special Acknowledgments

Until Today
Daily Devotions for Spiritual Growth and Peace of Mind
Iyanla Vanzant
A Fireside Book
Published by Simon & Schuster
Rockefeller Center
1230 Avenue of Americas
New York, NY 10020

Paving It Forward
Elisabeth Fayt
Morgan James Publishing
1225 Franklin Avenue, Suite 325
Garden City, New York 11530-1693

The Passion Test
Janet Bray Attwood
Chris Attwood
Hudson Street Press
375 Hudson Street
New York, NY

Spirit Seekers Publishing, Inc.
www.spiritseekerspublishing.com

"Whenever tragic loss occurs, you resist or you yield. Some people become bitter or deeply resentful; others become compassionate, wise, and loving."

—Eckhart Tolle

Introduction

When a woman discovers her husband is gay, she is confronted with many heart-wrenching emotions. Pain, hurt, anger, rejection, despair, helplessness, humility ... like a wild hurricane coming from all angles, these turbulent emotions can leave a person feeling raw, vulnerable, and exposed.

From personal experience, I am here to assure you that there is life after discovery. There is a way back to a sense of calm, peace, love, and joy. This book was written with that specific purpose in mind—to be a source of inspiration for women to focus on their healing and empowerment, to let them know that they do not need to live their lives wondering why, constantly questioning themselves, living with deceit and lies, walking on eggshells, or feeling inadequate.

When two people marry, we are led to believe that this special covenant signifies a lifelong relationship. But life has its twists and turns. It throws curves; things change, and people change. It is precisely the manner in which we cope with change that allows for growth and forward movement in our lives. There is a saying that reads, "Change is inevitable; growth is optional. Choose wisely." The truth is, we all live with change, and we all live with choices.

Traumatic upheaval in a relationship, especially a long-standing marital situation, is one of the most difficult experiences to come to terms with. One of the most important, fundamental truths that we must first come to understand, acknowledge, and fully embrace

1

in order to heal from any trauma is this: the quality of our lives corresponds directly to how we choose to react to the events that we encounter on a day-to-day basis.

It is important to remember that when you first connected with your spouse, when your relationship began, it served a purpose for you. Our relationships mirror ourselves and our needs.

When I look back to the time I met my first husband, it becomes easy to see that we were both a little "needy." In many ways, we did mirror each other. At the time, we were both on a similar emotional plane. That is why we were attracted to each other. At that time, we had a full relationship that was also sexually fulfilling. But as happens in many relationships, things changed. As I painstakingly learned to cope with those changes, I came to realize that change is part of the flow of life and that we all bear responsibility in the creation of our lives.

It is difficult at first to comprehend how we bring circumstances and people into our lives; but when we start to reflect on how our thoughts and our actions create the events of our lives, life definitely becomes more exciting. It was liberating for me, as I went through this process, to recognize how my thoughts and how my attitude about the events in my life affected the quality and the direction of my life. In so doing, I essentially became aware of the undeniable truth that my life starts and ends with me.

We often look outside of our lives to lay blame, to justify our decisions, or to explain that what is happening to us is out of our control. When we learn to take control of the direction, the path of our lives, we are better able to deal with the "stuff" that comes to the surface.

Finding out your husband is gay is seriously big stuff, but even within the context of the big stuff, it is vital to look within yourself to heal and to cope. Having lived through the experience myself, I know that it does take time to deal with the gravity of it all:

the discovery of your husband's sexuality, understanding how it is affecting you and your family, figuring out where to turn for support, and/or finding others who have successfully endured similar circumstances.

For wives of heterosexual adultery or heterosexual abuse or for women who are widowed, there are all kinds of support systems available. However, when a woman discovers her husband is gay, it is much more difficult to find support networks that deal with the healing process for the straight spouse. Most information available regarding homosexuality portrays the difficulties of being gay, while many of the homosexual avenues of support and resources focus mainly on the gay person coping with the coming-out process.

So where does the straight spouse go to find support and resources for her healing process? Unfortunately, even in this day and age, it is still more than likely that what is happening to the wife and family dealing with the disclosure of a homosexual husband and father is often left on the periphery; for the most part, they are left to cope on their own in a society that is not poised to handle these sensitive issues.

Healing is imperative if we are to move forward with our lives. In cases of gay spousal disclosure, healing involves being able to turn our focus from our spouse to ourselves, to refrain from dwelling on our hurt, to stop our pain and to look inside ourselves, to our spirit, for strength.

This book is about women, for women. It shares the emotions of distrust, betrayal, friendship, hurt, anger, and survival—not for "victims" to commiserate and wallow in, but to allow "victors" to see themselves for who they are. It is to allow them to rise above the circumstances and initiate hope and encouragement for a reawakening, a rejuvenation of one's self. More importantly, this book serves to give insights to forgiveness, to growth, to learning about one's self and living one's life with intent.

It is for all women everywhere, upon discovering their husbands are gay, to learn how to forgive, for them and for you. Learn to live your passion.

You ... Celebrate You!

Carolyn M. Brown

"The art of living lies less in eliminating our troubles than in growing with them."

—Bernard M. Baruch

> *"I was married for fifteen years before I found out my husband was gay. For the last year and a half, we went through counseling and the honeymoon phase that comes with it and stayed in the marriage for the children."*
>
> *Anonymous*

"*I was married for five years. A couple of years into our marriage, he disclosed that he was 'curious,' so we tried the swinger thing. This did not work. We later went to counseling. This did not work. Near the end of our marriage, he became less and less interested in me. I found credit card statements that indicated his other lifestyle. When I confronted him, he blamed me—said I was a bitch and blamed me for his choices. Like I was responsible for what he was doing! I deserve better.*

Anonymous

What's It All About?

There is much discussion and media attention on why, or why not, same-sex marriages should be allowed. It should be noted that homosexuals do marry; many, over the years, actually marry straight spouses. It has been presumed that if homosexuals were legally allowed to marry each other, it would alleviate the number of homosexuals marrying straight spouses. I'd like to believe that if society were more aware of these situations, maybe attitudes would change.

We cannot deny that homosexuality exists, and we cannot deny that children have been, and are, being raised in families where one parent is gay. Understandably, sexual orientation does not have a bearing on parenting ability. Homosexual as well as heterosexual parents have the ability to love and nurture children. A home where there is harmony and love is where a child will thrive.

Children are highly attuned to tension and stress; where sexual incompatibility exists, there is often tension and stress. When a straight spouse erroneously believes her partner is straight, inevitably the relationship suffers, and that adversely affects all those involved.

What most people are not aware of is that in today's society, there are a significant number of married men who are gay, who have children, and many who lead a double life. More disclosure and open discussion regarding gay-straight marriage relationships would, in my opinion, help alleviate the latent secrecy that currently shrouds this not-so-uncommon phenomenon.

When a gay man marries, there will come to be some point during the marriage when the fundamental nature of his orientation will begin to emerge. As the conflict of emotions increases within him over time, he will begin to feel constrained, and tension will build. At this point, if he has not already done so, he will start to look outside of the marriage for some form of acknowledgment or relief. This may be on the Internet or with casual social exchanges. As he begins to feel more comfortable in his other world, the conflict within himself and within the marriage will increase.

Movies such as *Brokeback Mountain* portray these circumstances as tragic love stories. The tragedy is seen as a love story, with the main male characters arranging secret rendezvous because society denies them the opportunity to openly express their sexual identity.

I agree no one should be denied their identity, their lifestyle, or the benefits of living in a free society. To my mind, the questions that really need to be addressed are: "Does the tragedy lie with the gay married man or does it lie with the wife and family he has deceived?" and, "Do these tragedies have to exist at all?"

Homosexuality itself is a multifaceted issue, but part of its "coming-out" process entails making the plights of the women and children suffering the deception of a gay spouse or father known and recognized for the often avoidable tragedy that they are.

> *"I understand what the women in the movie went through. I was married to a man who lived a secret life. The hurt and betrayal was indescribable. I feel sick that this story does not recognize the anguish of the women these men marry."*
>
> *Anonymous*

> *"We had been married for eleven years and had what looked like the perfect family. I finally understood that our married life was built on a falsehood. I felt as if I was standing alone with a big 'Stupid' sign stuck on my forehead."*
>
> *Anonymous*

"*The movie* Brokeback Mountain *turned a spotlight on gay men who lead double lives, having sex with other men while they are married to women. But that film didn't develop the story about the agony of the wives. When I saw the movie, I started to cry. I wanted to scream, 'This is a lie!'*"

Anonymous

As stated in the following excerpt used by permission from Iyanla Vanzant's book, *Until Today*, in the devotion for February 11:

I will know love when I realize ... people will come into my life for a reason, a season, or a lifetime!

Leaving just isn't easy! It is unfortunate and it happens. When it does we fight it because leaving someone you have spent time living with and loving is no easy task. In every relationship, regardless of how it started or how it is ending, there are so many good things you have convinced yourself could and should keep you together. They do, until the day you wake up and realize the things that once worked no longer do.

You know you've changed. You've grown. The little things that once brought a smile to your face are now a burden in your heart. You know what you have to do. You just don't know how to do it. You don't want anyone, especially you, to get hurt. You know that if you could just say what you feel, if you just move beyond the fear, the guilt, the anticipation of anger, you could close the door. It wouldn't be easy, but you could move on. You know you have done the best you could do. You know you have given all that you have to give. Yet for some reason, you keep on trying to make it work. Well, here is something you may not know—when you have learned all you can learn in a relationship, its season will end. When you have healed what you can into the relationship to heal, its purpose has been fulfilled. When a relationship is over, it's over! Hanging on will only make the days ahead darker!

Until today, you may have thought that ending a relationship was a difficult, challenging, or unnecessary experience. Just for today, be devoted to acknowledging and accepting all that you have learned and all that you have healed. When you can be grateful for those things, it will be easier to let go.

Today I am devoted to acknowledging lessons learned, blessings earned, and wounds that have been healed.[1]

---

1   Iyanla Vanzant, Until Today (New York: Simon and Schuster, 2007).

The Phoenix Rising—Coping with Change

According to Egyptian sources, a sacred bird was occasionally seen at the temple in Heliopolis, the city of the sun god. The bird symbolized the rising sun (i.e., the day and eternal rebirth). According to an Egyptian myth, Osiris transformed into a phoenix bird in Heliopolis. The bird was, from time to time, depicted sitting in a tree next to Osiris's coffin, thus symbolizing Osiris's—the dead man's—resurrection after death. In Greek sources, among others, Herodot, the phoenix bird's cyclic renewal, is a core theme.

Later authors have developed the story about the phoenix bird. Ovid and Mela told that the phoenix bird built itself a nest of incense and died in it. According to Artemidor, the bird burned in its nest made by incense and myrrh, after which a new phoenix bird emerged from the ashes. This story about the phoenix bird was spread and has lasted until today. Christian monks in the middle ages employed the phoenix bird as a symbol of Christ because of its voluntary death, its rebirth after death and its pure way of coming to life.[2]

---

2   accessed May 10, 2008, http://www.andersen.sdu.dk/forskning/motiver/vismotiv_e.html?id=70.

In the late 1980s, my ex-husband and I attended "The Phoenix Seminar" presented by popular motivational speaker Brian Tracy. This seminar was our introduction to being responsible for our lives. We learned about self-fulfilling prophecy and visualization and how to recognize and deal with our limiting beliefs.

This process did change our lives, for a while. There was a period where, as a family, we would rise every morning and listen to Brian's affirmation tape. We were aware of the power of visualization. We discovered how our past had influenced our present.

Then, somewhere along the way, we went back to living by default. We experienced life as it happened, falling into the rut of reaction instead of action.

Upon discovering my ex-husband was gay, I realized it was again time to become an active creator of my life. We are women who, like the phoenix bird, find rebirth and rise after the death of our marriages as we believe them to be. We are renewed in our faith. We have learned to let go of the situations in our lives over which we have no control. We understand we have no control over the actions of others. We will accept that others may, or may not, be there to support us. We take responsibility for our lives and only our lives. We acknowledge there are some things we will never understand. We address the pain we are feeling. We let go of our grievances. We forgive ourselves, and we forgive those who hurt us. We forgive, have closure, and move forward. We turn to our faith and our spirituality. We learn to become active creators in our lives.

Somewhere in your past, you met, you married, and you vowed before God, "Until death us do part ... forsaking all others." You may have had children. You may have experienced "through sickness and health ... for richer or poorer, for better or worse," finding out that "worse" is much more than you expected. You married, assuming and expecting your husband was heterosexual.

You believed the circumstances surrounding your dating relationship and marriage were as they appeared. You believed your love was based on heterosexual love. Then, one day, the facts were exposed, and your life was forever changed.

We are all familiar with the midlife crisis—the forty-something man who needs to reinvent his life where, all too often, reinventing means searching for new sexual excitement with other women. We do know if we awake one morning and find the love of our life is having an affair with another woman, as shattering as this may be to our self-esteem, there are avenues of support available. The tides are turned when, however, your husband not searching for another woman but rather for another man. Where do we turn to then?

As wives, we often feel ashamed to tell anyone.

Let us reflect on the word "shame," which is defined as "a strong emotion encompassing guilt and embarrassment."[3] As women who discover our husbands are gay, we should not feel guilty or embarrassed. Now you might say, "I do not feel guilty." However, if you are asking yourself, "How could I not have known?" that signifies guilt.

When we allow others to ask us that same question, we sometimes do not know how to respond. I have been asked, "How did you not know?"

My answer is, "Why and how would I have known? Our life together was sexual and mirrored that of other heterosexual couples around us."

Others also ask, "Are you sure? He can't really be gay." Again, this focuses responsibility on us. We hear how dreadful and sad it is that they (gay men) must suffer and hide their true selves, conforming to what society deems acceptable.

---

3   Yahoo Education, accessed March 28, 2009, http://education.yahoo.com/reference/dictionary/entry/shame.

What is sad is that society does not seem to grasp the gravity of what such a lie and such betrayal does to the straight spouse. When a gay man marries a woman, he is not honoring himself or his wife. This is not to say that he does not love the woman he married but rather that the union of marriage with a woman is not what is compatible with his inner feelings.

Once a woman becomes aware of his sexual identity, she then knows what the issue is and that something needs to change. But what do you do? How do you do it? As Elisabeth Fayt states in her book, *Paving It Forward*: "In looking for externals to change, we often fail to see what inside of us needs to change. When you ask that no circumstance in your life be changed … but rather for yourself to be changed … whatever inside of you needs changing will become known to you."[4]

You may say, "But it's not me who needs to change!" I suggest that by looking into yourself and what you need to change, you begin to heal and grow. You cannot change the circumstances, but you can change you.

Too often we fear change; we sometimes view the changing of ourselves as a negative, thinking something is wrong with us. The truth is, it is all about perspective. Change can be exciting and liberating. Change is one of the laws of the universe. The seasons change. People change. Change is constant, for everything is always changing.

When we grow up and leave home, we know going back will never be the same. When we left, we changed, and home changed.

And even our relationships change. Sometimes we grow together in our relationships, and sometimes we grow apart. The growing apart can be painful, but it does not have to be. We can choose to dwell on

---

4   Elisabeth Fayt, *Paving It Forward* (New York: Morgan James Publishing, 2009), 249.

pain, or we can choose to take it as an opportunity to re-create our life. Change can be exciting, and change can be about growth; it is all about how we choose to look at our circumstances. Our attitude and our thoughts determine the path our future will take.

We alone choose our thoughts; we can choose to be happy no matter what the circumstances. We are the active creators in our life whether we believe it or not. You might ask, "How can I feel happy with what has happened to me when my life, my world, has fallen apart? I thought I would be married forever."

The stark reality of today's society is that, for so many, marriages do not end in "happy ever after." Whether these relationships were heterosexual or not, they, too, have their story of pain and deception.

Many people are forced to deal with the death of a relationship. Yes, it is okay to mourn; it is necessary to grieve, to go through the process. The key is to go through the process and not to get stuck in the process. The longer you mourn and the longer you stay hurt and angry, the more imbedded these feelings become inside of you.

When you feel yourself wanting to cry, when you feel yourself wanting to tell your story, and when you feel yourself wanting to yell, take a moment and think about what made you happy in the relationship. Maybe it was the birth of a child, a wonderful vacation you shared, or a special holiday moment.

We can choose to remember the good or remember the bad. Happy thoughts serve you better. If you are not able to think happy thoughts, do something that makes you happy; find something that will make you laugh. Go to a movie, listen to a joke, or play some favorite music; notice how your energy shifts when you smile, when you choose to think happy thoughts.

We attract into our lives that which we think about. We can choose to think positive or negative thoughts, and our lives will reflect those thought patterns. Our thoughts are energy, we are energy, and we are surrounded by energy. The energy that surrounds us attracts circumstances and people of the same energy level. That is why your experiences reflect what you are thinking about.

So why not choose to think happy thoughts? Reflect on what was good about your relationship. Since we are constantly learning from our relationships, have appreciation for the lessons you learned from this one and know it served to make you a better, stronger individual.

There are many things I can look back on with gratitude. I have a family that I would not have had if not for this marriage. We had family vacations, holidays, and family experiences that provide us with fond memories. We can choose to focus on the good memories or the unpleasant memories. But why consciously choose to focus on what was unpleasant?

Remember the good! I am grateful for this marriage; if I had not experienced this event in my life, I would not be where I am today. This event caused me to expand my knowledge and to view the world in a different way. I am remarried and growing spiritually with my new husband, John. We have learned a great deal from each other and with each other through our ongoing studies and experiences. The phoenix rises to live again!

"I honor in you the Divine that I honor within myself and I know we are one."

—Deepak Chopra

Friends and Lovers

"I love you."

"You are my best friend."

"You are the most important person in the world to me."

These words are easy enough to say, but what do they really mean? Do they mean the same to both of you? Are the meanings harmonious with the roles in your relationship as you have defined them? I often hear women say, "He is my best friend. I love him so much."

Love is meant to be joyous, to enrich our lives, to enrich our spirit. Love is what we all search for. Love connects us. Does your relationship feel connected? Do you feel you are growing together or growing apart? Do you feel like best friends? Does your love feel spiritual?

Words like "best friend" are often used loosely. You may have thought you were best friends; however, best friends do not knowingly hurt each other. They are supposed to cherish one another, not hurt each other. Often, when the relationship is full of tension, neither person is treating the other like a friend.

I grew up under the auspices of the Golden Rule: "Always treat others the way you want to be treated." I applied this rule to my marriage, always giving to the relationship what I wanted to receive. What I found was that the more I tried, the more tension resulted. I was pushing the friendship, the lover aspect, too hard.

I realized that the more I tried to make situations romantic, the more tension developed. The more tension developed, the more we were not able to communicate. The energy level in our home became very low, with the vibration of tension permeating our relationship. There was a point where we probably were neither friends nor lovers.

We later became friends—people who share a past and a family. Because of that, we do care about what happens to each other. It is possible to maintain a friendship when you are able to let go and let your partner be who he is.

When we try to hold on to the relationship, molding it to be what we want it to be, we limit ourselves and our spouse from being who we are as individuals. It is necessary to be true to ourselves and allow our spouses to be true to themselves as well. That is the Law of Allowing. When we learn to allow, we eliminate the tension.

It is said it is difficult to be gay in this society and that it is not fair to expect the gay spouse to deny who he or she is. We, as straight spouses, did not ask our gay husbands to deny their sexuality, and they, in turn, should not expect us to deny ours. When the straight spouse does not know what the issue is, when we are led to believe there is something undesirable about us, we are being denied who we are and, as such, are not in a position to allow the gay spouse to be who he is.

If your life had evolved as planned, you would be best friends and lovers. However, life is what happens when we least expect it.

"The measure of a man's real character is what he would do if he knew he would never be found out."

—T. B. Macaulay

Trust, Love, and Relationships

Relationships are meant to be harmonious. Healthy relationships encompass many different aspects, including those of trust, honesty, thoughtfulness, communication, love, and compatibility, both spiritually and sexually. When a partner's sexual orientations are not compatible with those of his mate, it becomes more difficult to achieve harmony. Both partners in any relationship, whether they are gay or straight, deserve a relationship in which all aspects complement each other.

We expect our relationships to be built on trust and faithfulness. If the gay man reaches a time in his marriage when he feels he can no longer function happily in a heterosexual relationship, he should have the courage to come forward and end the relationship. Yes, it is difficult to be truthful, but the pain of lying is much greater to all those concerned.

Whether he comes to you of his own volition, telling you he is gay, or you discover the truth on your own, take the time to accept the truth.

In our situation, I was the one who made the discovery about my husband's sexual orientation; he did not come forward of his own volition. When I made the discovery, of course I was hurt and angry, but I was also relieved. I knew then that the tension in our marriage had nothing to do with me.

I did not confront him until the next day. I needed time to digest the information, and when I did confront him, he realized that the truth was finally out. It was a tearful situation but calm. At that time, I made a conscious decision not to hold onto anger. That does not mean I was never angry, just that I knew I would not hold on to the anger because that would hold me back.

Since that time, I have learned that it is important to allow others to be the people they were meant to be and for me to be the person I was meant to be. Allowing!

When you married, you thought your husband was heterosexual. He never told you he was gay; it was hidden. Whether he repressed those feelings or was actively living two lifestyles, you were denied the truth. You trusted the man you married.

Without a foundation of trust, relationships have little chance of success. Healthy relationships are based on trust and integrity. Oftentimes, when our trust is violated, we also act in distrusting ways. We spy, we search out, because we want to know what is going on. However, at the core level we, too, are acting in an untrusting way. Our actions mirror each other.

I realize that this is difficult to accept and that we have many ways to justify what we, as wives, are doing. In looking back, I realize that there was a great deal of pain associated with mistrust, with feeling the need to spy.

When trust is violated, we feel as if our lives are unraveling. This betrayal brings a terrible pain into our hearts. What we do with this pain determines our existence.

To be sure, it is necessary to go through the grieving process: to deny, to feel angry, to bargain, and to finally accept the situation. The process is not easy, but it is necessary, and it is one that does not need to, nor should it, go on for years.

Feel the pain to the core of your being. Feel it so intensely that you are able to lose your attachment to the pain. It is only by losing the attachment that we are free to grow.

"What do *you* want from *love*? What lies behind us, and what lies before us are tiny matters compared to what lies within us."
—Ralph Waldo Emerson

What is love? For all intents and purposes, within the context of this book and the issues being addressed, I am going to define love here as that state of being when the emotional security and well-being of your partner is as important to you as your own emotional security and well-being.

Does your marriage reflect this?

An intimate relationship is an interpersonal relationship combining emotional and physical intimacy, of which love is the basis.

So often, the word love is often used without ever substantiating what is meant by love. How many times have we heard, or even used the words, "I still love him," or "He still loves me"?

But what do these words really mean? While it may be true there is love in the relationship, it would be wise to ask yourself, "What type of love is it that we share?"

You can have different loving relationships with a variety of people. You love your God, your family, your children. You love your friends and those whose lives are an integral part of your life. With this love, there is no sexual desire. Then, there is passionate love—the love shown in an intimate relationship. When you have a passionate love, you express your love for each other sexually. You share life experiences, goals, beliefs, and values with that special person.

Yet whatever the love, whatever the relationship, the core of all love is the same. You want those you love to be happy; you want good things for them; you want others to treat them well. In turn, this means treating those you love with respect, but even more importantly, it means treating yourself with love and respect and having others treat you the same.

When you reflect on the aspects of love, ask yourself the following questions:

When I say I love someone, what type of love am I referring to?

Am I looking objectively at the reality of the situation in this moment, or am I guilty of looking at my love and life the way I thought it was?

Am I looking at my relationship in terms of the way I always thought it would be?

Am I looking at my relationship in terms of the way I want it to be?

Is the love I want from a marital situation a lifelong, intimate relationship, or rather that of a close friend?

Does this the love fulfill my desires emotionally and physically?

Is there appreciation in my relationship?

If we take a moment to really understand what a relationship is, we would discover that all relationships are special connections and, in the whole scheme of things, we are all connected. We all come from source energy and we are all connected through spirit.

Often, our personal relationships suffer because we have not, ourselves, connected to our God, our source. Sadly, most of us have the tendency to rely on relationships outside of ourselves to fill that void. When we understand and see the love spirit in ourselves, we are more open to sharing our love with others. Through love, we allow.

As we connect with our higher source, our God, we begin to see and understand how we are all connected. I know that as I have grown spiritually, I have come to realize that in order to have healthy, harmonious relationships and a healthy, harmonious life, I first needed to continue developing my connection and my relationship with God.

Over time, as I have worked with others facing similar challenges, I have seen the magnificent changes that come with connection to source. The deeper my silence and the deeper my times of connection, the more harmony and peacefulness I feel, the more I am attuned to the deep inner glow of love in my life. With this connection comes a deeper awareness that continually expands.

This connection within myself has led me to understand that as difficult as it may seem, whatever the relationship we are in at any given moment, it is exactly the right one for us at that time. We are connected to each other and are drawn to relationships because they are a match for us.

As stated before, our relationships mirror where we are in our life. When we are able to look at life with this connection, we are able to judge less and accept more. I am now able to understand that my relationship with my first husband was where I needed to be for me to learn what it was I needed to learn.

We are all energy; everything is energy. Our thoughts are energy and continuously emit a vibration attracting to us circumstances and people at a similar vibration level.

I understand now that when I met my first husband, our vibration levels were a match. That is why we were attracted to each other. I have also come to understand that as we shifted in different directions, our thoughts and our energy were no longer a match; the end of our marriage was not the end of our lives. New vibrations simply signified new beginnings.

With this in mind, you can now look at your life and your relationships in a different light. How have they changed? How have you changed?

We all have different expectations of our relationships, and these expectations shift as we evolve through life. What do you want from an intimate, loving relationship? What do you want from marriage? Does an intimate relationship for you consist of your best friend, lover, and monogamy all intertwined?

Only you can define what you need from your marriage. For me, marriage, intimacy, and spirituality are intertwined. Marriage is part of my spiritual journey. My husband, my lover, and my best friend are one and the same. In my new relationship, we are on the path, the journey together.

"Why do we, as women married to gay men, often react differently when our husbands are interested in men and not other women? If our husbands announced they could not be faithful and would prefer to be with other women, we would become angry and likely divorce them. Why is that we often think it is different when the affair is with a man—or when our husbands are looking at gay porn and chatting with other men? When he is caught looking at straight porn or chatting with women on the computer, it is usually considered infidelity. Is this because there is such a big deal made about 'their' struggle? No one is denying that same-sex attraction is a struggle, but ultimately, if a man is straight, bi, or gay and has an affair with anyone, it is adultery. If he is gay, he may need to live as a gay man and be involved with men. He should not be married and cheating on his wife."

Anonymous

> "There is nothing romantic about a secret affair, regardless of the sexual orientation. Having a homosexual relationship is not shameful, but having a secret relationship and living a lie is not right."
> Anonymous

"*I know you meant it when you said you loved me. I know you felt it, but it wasn't enough. I miss you and I know you miss me, too ... I know you never meant for it to be like this, not for me, not for you, and not for the children.*"

Anonymous

Why Do Gay Men Marry?

In the more recent literature and discussions regarding homosexuality, there is a common belief emerging that if this alternative lifestyle were more widely accepted and acknowledged, most gay men would not pretend to be heterosexual, marry, and have children. The fact remains, however, that even as society in general is becoming more accepting of homosexuality, young gay men are still marrying and having families. Why?

Reasons can be as varied as the men themselves, ranging from fear of being discovered, to denial/suppression of their innermost feelings, from fear of repercussions if anyone they knew found out, to sincerely wanting a family of their own.

Some men may feel they need to fit into society as a heterosexual, fitting more appropriately into the corporate structure; maybe they are uncertain and want the experience/comfort of a heterosexual relationship. Quite often, they actually do enjoy spending time with the woman they profess to love. And in most cases, they do love her; it is just not the sexually intimate love that one would associate within the sanctity of marriage, that soul connection of spirit and oneness.

Whether they are suppressing their homosexual feelings or are aware of them, they often feel their love will be enough to keep the marriage intact. Sadly, this often is not the case.

The fact is, if a gay man chooses to marry, leading a woman to believe he is heterosexual, he is making a choice. This choice will, inevitably, affect the direction of not only his life, but also of hers and those of any children they might have.

According to www.marriedgay.org,[5] there are a variety of reasons that gay married men don't acknowledge themselves as gay; most of those reasons relate to fear:

Fear that they will lose their wife, her love, and friendship;
Fear they will lose their children;
Fear they may have exposed their wives to health issues.

Many of these fears tend to focus on their means of coping, and have nothing to do with their wife's feelings or the trust they are breaking. Even when they are caught with factual evidence, many will still proclaim their innocence; they find excuses, justify, or shift blame.

The fact remains, we all have a choice on whether to marry. It is necessary to keep in perspective the difference between having control and choice over actions vs. having no choice at all.

Many gay married men will openly admit that they run into serious difficulty trying to maintain their role sexually in a marriage while sustaining their sexual activity with male partners. Once the burden of secrecy is lifted, when the truth is finally revealed, the gay partner's liberation often becomes their wife's pain. The fear, guilt, and shame can, in the blink of an eye, be transferred from one marital partner to the other.

By the time their marriage reaches this point, no matter what options the couple tries to pursue, most will eventually end up divorcing each other. Often, the longer it takes for the marriage to dissolve, the greater the emotional cost for both parties. In some cases, partners may or may not have a part in the decision of whether or not to stay married. Sometimes they are just left.

---

5   How often has it been said......? *"They can't be gay, they are married!"*? You would be surprised! Or would you?, accessed February 15, 2009, http://www.marriedgay.org/beforeumarry.html.

"He just wouldn't admit he was gay. We struggled with this issue at therapy. I had to learn, as other women did, to find my own truth. Just because he doesn't admit it to himself or me does not mean it is not true. I figured this out when the therapist told me, 'If he was an alcoholic and did not admit it to himself, does this mean he is not an alcoholic? No, it just means he is in denial.' It would just be easier for me to move on if he could look me in the eye and say he was sorry for putting my life in his drama and lies. It is not fair that he used me this way and even worse that he decided to selfishly bring our children into this world knowing that he would be living this lie."

Anonymous

Uncovering the Truth

It is often said, "He can't be gay; he is married and he has children." Truth be told, there are many married gay men. Some have come out of the closet and some have not. Some gay husbands are honest and disclose the truth to their wives. Others just leave without any explanation.

Often we, as wives, have to search for the truth ourselves. Many women follow the trail of "clues" and then confront their gay husbands with the facts. Even with the facts uncovered, many men will still deny the truth. The path to discovery can be painful but, in retrospect, not nearly as painful as living with the constant lies and deceit.

So where exactly does it all start? What leads a wife to even consider that her husband might be gay? Usually, our intuition kicks in first, telling us something is wrong. We just can't pinpoint it, but as the clues become more obvious, we start to actively search for the truth.

There really is no fool-proof method in unmasking your partner's secrets. You can guess; you can ask him; he can tell you; or you just discover it by the tracks he leaves behind. I have added the following information for women who struggle with finding out the truth. We often feel the need to know before we can accept what it is we discover.

According to http://marriedgay.org/excuses.html (January 16, 2009), the following are some excuses you may hear when you confront your husband. Keep in mind they are general responses and are by no means definitive.

When found to have a collection of compact discs with pornographic pictures on them: "Don't you remember that I bought a batch of second-hand discs, which I had been assured had been formatted?"

When discovered having condoms and lube in his work bag: "Some guys at work must have put them there as a joke!"

When discovered with gay links on his computer: "I have no idea how they got there—someone else must have put them on my machine." A variation on this one is, "A hacker must have put them on there!"

When discovered with gay porn on his computer, he tries to say that it was on the cookies as a result of pop-ups from another website.

When found to have "crabs": "I must have picked them up from bed sheets in that hotel I stayed in a few days or weeks ago!"

When confronted with the truth, he tries to turn it around on his spouse and make her look like the guilty party.

When found with sexually explicit messages on his phone from another man: "It was just a prank by a mate at work."

When on the phone to his boyfriend late at night, "Oh, it's only my boss."

When discovered with a magazine with pictures of naked men, "Oh, I was just comparing their penis size with my own."[6]

The Internet is full of websites, chat rooms, and personal ads for presumably "happily married men" posting their profiles online

---

6   Excuses, excuses, accessed February 15, 2009, http://marriedgay.org/excuses.html

in search of "discreet encounters" with other men. There are also forums providing information for women on how to discover what their husbands are searching for on the Internet. A computer search will often reveal the gay pornography sites, the personal ads reviewed and researched, and any e-mails to would-be lovers.

Unfortunately, for many wives, this is the manner in which the truth is uncovered.

In the Light of Discovery

The discovery of one's husband being gay, whether voluntary or not, is nothing short of tumultuous and overwhelming. We watch as life as we knew it uncontrollably unravels. At this time, it is easy for us to totally lose direction, to lose focus, to become caught up in the pain and despair. We are confused, angry, and hurt. Support groups dealing with the issue of homosexuality direct us toward what it means to be gay in today's society and focus on the stress our spouse must be going through. And in all that, we forget to ask ourselves, "What is it I am feeling?" and "What is it that I want?"

How discovery affects our present and our future depends on how we choose to react in the light of the discovery. If we look at discovery in the context of finding out the truth, of unearthing something terrible, we remain in pain. If we choose to look at discovery as a breakthrough, we can then start the path of healing and creating our life.

I do not mean to minimize the pain but rather to reinforce that it is necessary to grow through the pain and to understand that even when something terrible happens, we need to be open to something wonderful taking its place. There is a flow to life. As the Bible says, "There is a season for everything."

Choose to view discovery as something positive in your life. You now know what the issues are. You are now free to make decisions based on your new knowledge. Where are you going to place your energy? Will you let your thoughts and actions move you forward?

Again, the more energy you give to the negative, hurtful aspects of this discovery, the more pain you will attract to your life. In my experience, the discovery itself was very difficult and very painful, but at the same time extremely freeing. I knew I had not been crazy; there was something wrong with us, and it was nothing I could fix.

It has been said when the straight spouse discovers the truth regarding her husband's sexual orientation, she retreats to the closet. For me initially, it was the "secret" in our family. I now see how damaging that was, even keeping the secret for just a short time.

When we go into the closet, we do not heal. We may find that when we try to open the door of our closet, just a little bit, we feel compelled to quickly shut it again. The support we are looking for just is not there, and sometimes people just don't know how to react. People may ask:

"Are you sure?"
"How could you not know?"
"It can't be; he loves you so much."
"It's the media today; they are trying to make this lifestyle acceptable."
"Has he changed his mind?"
"Is he coming back?"

When I was constantly bombarded with these questions, my first reaction was to return to my "closet." Over time, I found it became easier to disclose this information and speak openly about it.

Homosexuality affects more families than I was aware of at that time. We truly are not alone. I met individuals who had a gay brother or sister. I met others who had also been married to someone gay. Or there were those who had a brother or sister who had been married to someone gay. We do not need to hide, even though we may feel we have many reasons.

Of all the reasons we try to hide behind, shame often tops the list. We are afraid people will think we were "stupid"; there must have been clues. We worry that people will think we weren't a good enough partner, that it was our lack of love and understanding that drove our partner to seek an alternative lifestyle.

Other reasons we tend to keep our "secret" to ourselves include:

We are afraid of the talk and the gossip.
We are afraid of reactions.
We are just afraid.

Fear is paralyzing and holds us back. Fear is worry, and worry is a negative and incredibly destructive emotion. Destructive fear increases stress and hinders our decision-making process. Fear drains us of positive energy. When we are negative, we cannot access our joy. There comes a time when we gradually must leave the closet and release the pain. Fear and negative emotions/feelings are not in alignment with a joyful life.

What would you do if you had no fear? We often stay "stuck" because of fear. The quicker you let go of fear, the sooner you can enter a new phase of your life. To overcome fear, have faith. Fear is the opposite of faith. Fear and faith are not compatible emotions. Remember, whatever it is you focus your attention on, grows stronger. Do not focus on your fear, but rather focus on how you want the relationships in your life to be—what you believe you can achieve.

Upon discovery/disclosure, some women choose to be vengeful, wanting to "out" their spouse. Please do not take this path! Leave your closet as a means of acknowledging that this part of your life;

it is how you arrived at where you are now. The fact is that you were once, or still are, married to someone gay. That will always be a part of your reality. Being vindictive will cause you to hold onto the hurt. When you are not vindictive in your actions, you free yourself.

"Holding on to anger is like grasping a hot coal with the intent of throwing it at someone else. You are the one who gets burned."

—Buddha

When we are comfortable coming out of the closet, we are better able to garner support. It took a long time for me to finally confide in a close friend. I felt that because I had known her forever she would know, without any explanation, that I was getting divorced for a very good reason. When I finally told her the truth, she responded by saying, "How could I help you when I didn't know?" Then it made perfect sense. I did not need to be afraid to tell.

You may or may not want to share your story. If you do share your story, state it and move on. Do not hold on to your pain. Embracing the drama in our lives usually leads to bitterness and negativity. In order to heal, fill your life with things and people you enjoy. Positive thoughts, feelings, and emotions are the foundation for happiness.

When I could finally openly admit that, yes, my husband was gay, I wanted information on how other women in this situation coped. I searched bookstores, purchased and read books, and searched the Internet for information. I read about homosexuality, open marriage, and sexual fluidity. I could not find what I was searching for—information directed at healing the straight spouse; and this led me to the conclusion that there was not a great deal of support or information available to adequately meet the needs of the straight spouse.

Ironically, by the time you find out your husband is gay, he has already been part of a support group, chatting on the Internet, meeting gay friends, etc. He realizes that he is not alone; he realizes there are other gay married men experiencing what he is experiencing and there is support for him to free himself of his burden. These avenues have helped him recognize where he is comfortable. There are gay support groups, gay activists, and events covered by the media to promote the acceptance of gay rights. These events are separate and should not become entangled in the emotions a woman goes through in dealing with the discovery that her husband is cheating, and yes, her husband is also gay. When we find out, it is important to find support and comfort as soon as possible.

In the emotional state of feeling lost and alone, most wives will turn to turn to the Internet as a source of support. There are sites where options are offered to try to make the marriage work. Invariably, many sites offer support to the oppressed gay male. Often these sites focus on his being gay and not the recovery of the straight spouse. On these sites there is much discussion about how he was "caught," the actions of being gay, what he has done, the lies he has told, and the lies he is still telling.

Fortunately, there are also sites where women share their stories, although many of these stories are told with a great deal of pain, hurt, and anger. These sites provide a venue where we find we are not alone and we can share our thoughts and feelings.

While it is helpful to have an avenue to share stories and learn that others have similar experiences, it is also necessary to not let this become a focal point of your life. In order to cope and grow, it is necessary to focus on you—to realize that his being gay does not excuse betrayal and to realize that his being gay has nothing to do with you. It is also necessary to understand how your thoughts and actions affect your life. The more you play out the drama, the more drama you will attract. We attract to our lives that which we give attention to.

After my discovery, I found it extremely helpful to search through the works of Dr. Wayne Dyer and Dr. Deepak Chopra. This helped me to take focus away from the pain and to focus on my growth and spiritual path. As stated before, we had at one time started the path of self-discovery together, attending and studying the works of Brian Tracy, Zig Ziglar, Dale Carnegie, Anthony Robbins, and others. We understood about "self-fulfilling prophecy." I am now grateful for the discovery, as it brought me back to my spiritual and personal growth.

Through this traumatic time in my life, I spent a fair amount of time in meditation and introspection, trying to gain insight into my life and how I had arrived at this point. We had married two weeks after my twentieth birthday and had only dated for four months. We really didn't know enough about each other and had not experienced the maturity life experience brings. By the time I turned twenty-three, we had two children. Like all marriages, we had our ups and downs. There were times I felt that marriage really should not have to be hard work; love, life, and relationships are meant to be enriching and not painful.

Love is not about work. Life is not about work. Work is something accomplished through effort. Our lives are created through the energy of vibration from our thoughts, words, emotions, and feelings. The more we are aware of how our thoughts and actions affect our vibration and what we attract, the more we understand that we get what we think about, whether we want it or not, harmonious relationships included. It is all about where we place the attention in our relationships and what we focus on.

We can create harmony or disharmony in our lives. Prior to the time of discovering the truth, there is usually conflict within the household. It may be below the surface, or everyone in the house might be aware of the tension. At this point, each spouse is mirroring their distrust and their unhappiness. When there is tension in the marriage, both partners are emitting a low frequency of energy surrounding them. The resistance to what is happening in our lives causes tension, disharmony, and often disease.

When we are able to accept what is happening, when we are able to allow, we create more harmony in our life. When we understand that our relationships mirror ourselves, we can create more harmony. We can learn to be accepting, loving, and forgiving. We can turn the discovery into something positive.

How you react, how you come to terms with the discovery will have an impact on the lives of other members of the family as well, especially any children you might have had together. Children sense when things are not right. They might think you are only having the usual marital conflicts, but they will sense something. If you want harmony in your life, you must be authentic with yourself and with your children. Being authentic is when what you think, what you do, and what you say is in alignment with who you are. Your children deserve authenticity. Your relationships deserve authenticity. Show up in your life and your relationships as who you truly are.

Crisis Management

When you discover your husband is gay, you are faced with life-changing decisions. Regardless of how long you have been married, the process of disclosure is devastating. This deception leaves many wives feeling that their marriage was a lie. Take time to reflect. Yes, you were lied to, but your marriage was not a lie.

To move through this period of crisis, it is necessary to make appropriate and effective decisions. Remember, the situation will keep changing, so take steps to prevent the crisis from escalating. You may start asking yourself, "How could it get any worse?"

The more time you spend reviewing your options, analyzing the situation, checking up on what your gay spouse is up to, the more you are adding to your stress. You are sending out negative vibrations that, in turn, will bring you more circumstances to be unhappy about.

It is not your responsibility to judge another's actions; however, it is your responsibility to determine how you will let those actions affect you.

This is not to say that I didn't have my times of anger, my times of tears. I went through the process of grieving. I just didn't want to remain in the process. I made what could be called "mistakes." However, even since that time, I have learned there are no mistakes; I just look at them, now, as "tuition." Yes, life is full of lessons; we can grow from our circumstances and experiences, or stagnate with them. Trust yourself; you are capable of growing with and through the circumstances of your life.

During the period following the discovery, my ex-husband and I entered counseling. I was surprised at the options presented at counseling and in some of the books I read. These options were entirely different than those presented to a heterosexual couple trying to overcome the issue of a cheating spouse.

One of the options presented was that of an open marriage. For me, an open marriage was not a consideration, as it did not reflect my values. Not only that, the secrecy, health, and trust issues related to such an arrangement did not bode well with me, either.

If you should decide to consider the open marriage option, remember that the parameters often keep expanding, with the terms being renegotiated. In most cases, it will not be any easier to openly have this new arrangement than when he was living a secret life. Questions to ask yourself before considering an open marriage arrangement are:

Is sex important to me?
Do I want to negotiate the sexuality and the intimacy in my marriage?
Do I want a life of secrecy and doubt?
Will these arrangements allow me to trust?
Will they bring joy to my life?

For couples who do open their marriage to other relationships, more often than not, the couples end up divorcing. One must ask the question, "How often is a wife in a heterosexual marriage offered this option when she discovers her straight husband is unfaithful?" Not often. So, we need to ask ourselves, "Why is it we are given this option?"

According to the Straight Spouse Network, it is estimated there are up to two million Mixed-Orientation Marriages (MOM) where one spouse is either gay, lesbian, bisexual, or transgendered. Statistics from this network claim, "When the gay, lesbian, or bisexual spouse comes out, a third of the couples break up immediately; another third stay together for one to two years, sorting out what to do and then divorce. The remaining third try to make their marriages work. Half of these couples divorce, while half of them (17 percent of the total) stay together for three or more years."[7]

You may be told you are insecure for wanting monogamy. Please remember that insecurity and having a value system are entirely different. Individuals have different value systems. You are still a heterosexual woman with the same needs and desires you had before you found out he was gay. It is not necessary for you to compromise your beliefs and values. You do not need to redefine what you want from a relationship because he is gay. You can remain friends without being in a mixed-orientation marriage.

Many people find it difficult, if not impossible, to share their spouse. For me, sharing was not part of the vows we made when we were married. It is possible to have a relationship with him as a friend and to support him as a friend. You don't have to be a spouse to be a friend.

---

7   Aboutcom.marriage— Straight Spouses — What to Do and What Not to Do If Your Spouse is Gay, accessed January 29, 2009, http://marriage.about.com/cs/straightspouses/a/straightspouse.htm.

"An open marriage is nature's way of telling you that you need a divorce."

—Ann Landers

I expected to maintain a good relationship with my ex-husband, even though I knew we would be divorced. This is because I intended it to be that way. As a result, we have maintained an amicable relationship. We spent many years together, had grown children, and have grandchildren. Even though I was devastated, I was not about to become bitter. I realized bitterness leads to a hardening of the heart. With that hardening, a small part of you dies. It is important to "allow."

Sometimes it is necessary to let go of a relationship that no longer serves us. This does not mean we do not cherish what this relationship brought us at the time, but rather, we recognize that we have learned all we can and it is time to move on, to develop the other relationships in our lives, beginning with our relationship with God and with ourselves.

When living together becomes an effort, whether the relationship is heterosexual or when one spouse is gay, the issues need to be addressed as the marriage is either close to, or already in, crisis mode. Any marriage in crisis mode has options. You may stay or you may go. Some questions you need to ask yourself are:

"What are my expectations?"

"How am I willing to redefine my marriage, my vision, and my goals?"

"Is monogamy important to me?"

"Can I trust him?"

"What are the consequences if nothing changes?"

"Has my health been compromised?" (Even if he tells you he has been faithful, have yourself checked for sexually transmitted diseases and HIV.)

"What is my financial situation?" Has he been open and honest about my financial resources? (You have entitlements.)

"Can my emotional well-being withstand the possibility of sharing him sexually and emotionally with another man? "

Remember, homosexuality is not just about sex. Orientation is the core of who the person is, and this information needs to be taken into account when making decisions that affect the rest of your life. Counseling is available, and it is wise to seek it. I would recommend, however, that when searching for a counselor, you find someone whose views and values reflect yours. I found it helpful to interview the counselor before deciding to hire one.

When deciding whether or not to file for divorce, someone once said they calculated how many weekends they might have left in their life and decided they didn't want to spend them with the same person in the same way anymore. Assess your situation: "How do you want to spend the rest of your life?" Be careful not to overanalyze; "paralysis through analysis" stops forward movement. When reviewing your options, use the following steps to assist in the decision-making process:

"What information is relevant, and what information is not?"
"What is fact-based, and what is not?"
"Are financial considerations playing a role in my decision?"
"What are the possible implications of my options?"
"What are the impacts on myself and others affected by my decision?"

If you are considering staying in the marriage, you need to have a clear understanding of what you will tolerate and what you won't. In order for any marriage to work, there must be trust; you must both want to work on it together, and you must both agree when it is time to seek counseling or to stop counseling. Define the "deal breakers" and what is best for you. Do you want your husband to change? Do you want a conflict-free environment? Do you want a more satisfying sex life?

You need to know when to say, "I will not allow myself to be treated like this anymore." It is important to recognize that the first time you are hurt may not necessarily be your responsibility, but if you continue to let it happen, then you alone are accountable.

Again, we teach others how to treat us by how we treat ourselves. Ask yourself if the options you are considering will make you happy. Here are some questions to ask:

"How do I feel when we are together?"
"How do I feel when he is away from home?"
"How do I feel when I know he is coming home?"
"When we are together, is there passion?"
"Does he have and/or show empathy and compassion?"
"Do we share our spirituality?"

When you allow yourself to continually live with pain, you move further away from the life you desire. Many women have sacrificed their dreams and the possibilities life may have had to offer for what they considered "security."

Relationships do not have to be about sacrifice. Sacrifice is about giving things up. There is no need to give up the values that are the core of your essence. Compromise and sacrifice are different. In compromise, you are meeting each other halfway by giving things up that are okay with you. Maybe you decide one person cooks and the other person cleans; this is compromise. When you sacrifice, you are surrendering what is important to you. You do not need to sacrifice. Follow the path that will lead you to the life you deserve.

Be honest with yourself and listen to what your intuition is telling you. Whenever you are faced with a choice, ask yourself:

"What decision will bring joy to my life?"
"What decision is in alignment with my goals?"
"What decision is in alignment with what I feel passionate about?

Follow your heart and follow your passion. Do what feels right for you. Create the life you want to live.

You may, or may not, choose to marry again. I knew I wanted to remarry. I enjoy a loving relationship. I enjoy the sharing and caring. I enjoy growing together. I had a list of what I wanted in a relationship, what I wanted from love. I gained a valuable lesson, though, in deciding to rediscover love; I learned not to move forward too quickly. I started dating too soon. It takes a while for your vibration level to change. You have to give yourself time to shed the energy associated with the relationship you are leaving behind. When I was fully able to appreciate myself, what my marriage had brought me, to redefine my friendship with my ex-husband, I was then able to attract more goodness, and the love I desired, into my life.

It is perfectly natural to want to be loved. Our yearning for love is a yearning to be connected with spirit, to be connected with our source. I have observed in others, and learned from my own experience, that being disconnected with our source leaves our lives disconnected. The connection with source is pure love.

I have also learned that to grow spiritually and to have a fulfilling relationship with another, you must both be on the same spiritual path. To determine your connection with source and what you are searching for in your relationship(s), ask yourself the following:

"How are the relationships in my life?"
"How is my relationship with myself?"
"Am I a spiritual person?"
"Are my work or family relationships fulfilling?"

If you feel there is a consistent pattern in what you are (or are not) receiving from your relationships, look at your relationship with yourself. How do you treat you? It is important to understand that we teach others how to treat us. When we allow others to treat us badly, we are sending a message that we do not feel we deserve to be treated well. Do you berate yourself with internal dialogue that is critical and demeaning?

"How could I be so stupid?"
"I must be very unattractive."
"If I wasn't so fat, men would treat me better."
"If I was smarter, I could find a good man."
"If I had stayed in the workforce, I could support myself."

Start telling yourself that you deserve the best. You can change your inner dialogue. Treat yourself well. Have quiet time, have that bubble bath, listen to music you enjoy, read. Learn to love yourself. And above all that, have faith; life and love can be what you want them to be. Your life is waiting for you to create it. Learn to love yourself and appreciate the relationships you have. Give to your relationships what you want to receive. The more you appreciate what you had in your relationship, what you have in your present relationships, what you appreciate about your life, the more you will find yourself attracting people to you who will support and love you.

> *"It is really the secrecy and cheating. The wife, too often, is rejected sexually on a continual basis, and this is very damaging. It should be about treating each other with respect and appreciation."*
> *Anonymous*

"I filed for bankruptcy shortly after we divorced. I had been on antidepressants, and they weren't working. I needed him to leave. After he moved out, I went back to school, repaired my credit, and fell in love again. My ex and I still talk; there are the children. The pain hurts, but life gets better ... gets really better."

Anonymous

> "Being gay is not the problem. A person does not 'get over' being gay any more than a person 'gets over' being straight. A gay man in a monogamous marriage will likely spend his life pretending to be someone he is not—a straight man. Would you stay in a monogamous marriage-type relationship even with your [female] best friend when you are not a lesbian?"
>
> *Anonymous*

"When we cling to pain, we end up punishing ourselves."

—Leo Buscaglia

Telling the Children

The healing process is difficult for all members of the family. At some point, the news will need to be shared with the children. Depending on their ages and the circumstances, the manner in which you choose to tell them, and when, will differ. There is no one right way to broach the subject. Whether or not we do it the right way, or what may be perceived as the wrong way, we do it with love for our children as the main concern.

It is my view that children be given information appropriate to their age and level of understanding. Secrets are never good. I believe the truth always comes out and usually in ways that are much more devastating than if the truth was shared in a caring, loving manner.

It is said that young children are adaptable. However, as adults, we often do not give them the choice. We force the consequences of our choices on them. They have to adapt. We may lovingly assist them in adapting, but the circumstances are not of their choosing. Younger children may say everything is okay, but they all face difficulties. They may be ridiculed at school. If they are teenagers, they may be embarrassed. Keep an open dialogue, and never criticize or belittle their father. Teach them the law of allowing. When we allow, we do not feel distress.

We hear that older, adult children are busy with their own lives and capable of understanding. Older children of divorced parents, regardless of the reason for the divorce, often feel their family life has been a lie. Adding homosexuality to the issue increases the internal conflict.

The following, written by an adult child, shows an aching heart; this is the reality:

"Well, I am not too sure what to say right now. I am feeling like someone close to me has just died. The life and family that I had is gone. It will never be the same, and that makes me sad. I just feel completely crushed. I thought that last night [night of disclosure] was just a nightmare that would just go away. Why did my perfect family have to end up like this? On the way to work this morning, I broke down and I started crying. I don't know why this had to happen, and I don't know what will happen now. Well, that's all for now—I wish I could give you a hug [to the mother] because I know you are as scared as I am."

Anonymous

Offer your children the support necessary to assist them in overcoming this trauma. Finding a good counselor to help them through the process is a starting point. Do not undermine their father; he is still their father, and if they had a good relationship prior, you should not try to harm this. If it was not a good relationship, there are more emotions that will need to be addressed.

Remember, children feel the pain, children feel hurt; they too are victims of deceit. Teach your children how their thoughts and actions create their life. Help them find their connection to source. Help them remember what is good, what makes them happy; provide them with thoughts that put a smile on their face. Help them develop an aura of happiness emitting strong vibrations. Use this as an opportunity to teach them about the laws of the universe, to introduce them to meditation and spiritual growth.

"I was married for seventeen years to a man before I found out he liked men as well as women. At this point, he told me he had been with a guy even before we met. I had thought he was my soul mate. He knew the one thing I hated most was being lied to, and what a lie we lived. Of course, this hurt me a lot. I tried to keep the marriage together. I had a five-year-old and a baby. I turned from a loving, caring woman to someone who was angry and could not trust."

Anonymous

"It is so easy to stay in denial, anger, and hurt. It is only by moving through those emotions that we can heal ourselves. Sometimes it is a wonderful journey, and other times it is painful and exhausting but worth it! I later accepted that many of my own issues were also hidden in the relationship. There were things from my past that I thought I had healed but had only been covered up in my marriage. I've been there, I've spied, I've cried. I've presented the evidence and had it explained away ... we don't want to be spies, we want the truth. When I finally woke up, quit the spying, quit the crying, I realized ... despite his excuses, he was not going to change. I moved to acceptance, looking at the facts in order to move toward healing. I understood that my obsession with his behavior was stopping me from healing."

Anonymous

Healing

It is a fact—you and your husband have shared a history together. It may be a long history, or it may be relatively short. Regardless, the hurt is deep. Do not view your past life together as a lie. It was real. Any joys you shared were real; any difficulties were real. Your family experiences were real.

You had reasonable expectations from your marriage, and they were violated. You lived your life the best you could with the knowledge you had. You now have new knowledge, and you must not ignore the realities. What you do with your new knowledge is your responsibility, as the decisions you make will impact your life. Sometimes we are guilty of disregarding the new knowledge. We put a spin on what is happening, trying to make it more palatable.

You do need to take time to heal. It is necessary to change your energy from one of hurt to one of optimism. You can do this by not living in the past. Your life is a journey, and you are about to explore new trails that will lead you somewhere magnificent, if only you believe.

How do you get rid of the hurt, of the pain? Experience your pain, cry, go to the depth of your pain, feel it at your core, and then release it. Feel your pain to its depths—all your regrets, your sorrow, your anger. Pain is something we will all experience. What we choose to do with our pain is up to us. Once the pain is released, we are able to change our thoughts to ones that bring us joy or pleasure. We need to be aware of our feelings; our feelings tell us what we are thinking about. When we notice a feeling of sadness, we can learn to shift our thoughts to ones that will make us smile. When we smile, our energy instantly shifts.

When I am aware that I need an "energy shift," I think of, or look at pictures of, my grandsons. The younger one, the baby, radiates love and a spirit that is still connected to God; the older grandson provides me with many wonderful memories of time spent together. I see the love and joy he experiences with those he loves without focusing on the trials of growing up.

What thoughts bring you joy? What makes you smile? When you think of that which brings you joy, or what makes you laugh, you will feel your energy shift. Remember, we control our thoughts and feelings. When we change our thoughts, when we change our feelings, we, in turn, change our lives. When we feel good, our vibrations are high, and we are able to attract more of what we want into our lives.

So how does one go about the process of healing? To heal, you need to learn to love yourself. It is not selfish to love yourself. Loving yourself is critical to your success and happiness. Just as the flight attendant instructs us to first put the oxygen mask on ourselves in case of emergency, we, too, must nurture and love ourselves before we are fully able to nurture others.

To learn to love ourselves, we need to reprogram our subconscious. Our subconscious has a belief system that was developed from childhood by the input provided from others. Our young minds were like sponges taking in what others said. Sometimes these were negative statements that made us feel we were not worthy—that we did not look good enough, or we were not smart enough. These statements could have been from our parents, our teachers, our siblings, or our friends, and as we got older, they might have come from our relationships.

It is important to recognize that these statements were and are not facts, but rather the opinions of others. Our conscious mind feeds everything to our subconscious mind. The subconscious mind is where our values and beliefs are developed. Our subconscious does not know what is real and what is not. It takes what it hears and believes it. These untrue statements, fed into your subconscious, developed your belief system. "I'm not good enough." "I'm not smart enough." "I'm not attractive enough."

Remember, your thoughts create everything in your life, including your beliefs. So why not feed your subconscious with statements that will bring joy to your life? One way of accomplishing this is by affirmations. For affirmations to work, we need to believe our affirmations and repeat them often. Repetition will cause the subconscious to reprogram more quickly.

As Elisabeth Fayt writes in *Paving It Forward*, "When you know the energy behind what thoughts do to your life, you get very motivated to make a change for the positive."

Elisabeth created an incredibly effective system called pre-paving™ that consciously enables everyone to live a life of intent. In her words, she proposes:

"Make pre-paving™ a habit. Pre-paving™ is consciously choosing your thoughts and words to create your life experiences. Set your intentions for the day each morning, give gratitude throughout the day and end your day with intention and gratitude. Give gratitude and appreciation for the relationships you have, the beauty that surrounds you, for family, health, and friends. Focus on your healing. A pre-pave™ for the change that is going on in your life could be "I am becoming the person I want to be."[8]

---

8   Elisabeth Fayt, *Paving It Forward* (New York: Morgan James Publishing, 2009), 11.

So take some time to reflect on your life. In order to make sound judgments, get to the heart of what matters. Deal with what is, not what you think it should be. You do have a choice on how you think, how you feel, on how you act or react. You cannot move forward if you continue to reflect and live in the past. The present is a gift; it is ours today.

As we grow, how we reflect on our past will change. Over time, the intensity we feel about what has happened shifts, so we need to live in the present. The moment we are in is the moment we are to experience. Accept things as they are in this moment, and be aware that you have the ability to choose the direction your life will now take. Life is a journey, a path, and you choose your direction.

Envision your future, what you want it to look and feel like. Move forward.

"If you focus on what you've left behind, you will never be able to see what lies ahead. Pre-pave™ a fresh start to consciously release the past."

Elisabeth Fayt

Letting Go

When you know the truth for what it is, it is much easier to accept it and do what is best for you. Letting go and moving on does not mean you have failed. It means you are opening yourself up to a new life and allowing your partner the freedom to move on to create his life.

Before you can move forward, it is necessary to accept the reality of your present life and have the desire to change. It is possible to get comfortable in a toxic environment. Some wives stay because they want to prove they could "stick it out." Some stay because they truly believe the relationship will get better and stay better. Some stay because they are afraid.

There is only one real choice: stay if it makes you feel good; when it is what makes you happy. Marriage is about commitment, intimacy, love, and trust. You do not need to settle for less.

Recognize when it is time to change and when it is time to let go. You need to change your perspective and see beyond your problems and focus on your ability to successfully move your way through this challenging situation. Realize it takes time to change. Adapt to change. Not adapting does not make it any easier. You have more strength than you realize.

First, let go of the anger; let go of the hurt. Recognize your anger. You are angry at him, and you are probably angry at yourself, thinking you should have recognized some signs. Sometimes there are no signs; sometimes we are unable to face the signs. Whatever the reason, it does not matter. There is no benefit to holding on to anger. When we let go of the anger, we can forgive.

Forgiveness

You might say, "How can I forgive?" Very simply—forgive now! Forgive him, and also forgive yourself. You don't have to forgive him for him; forgive him for you. Forgive yourself for judging, forgive yourself for feeling you have made poor choices, and forgive him for causing you pain. Forgive the hurt he has caused you. Forgive him for being critical of you. Forgive yourself in all areas where you are beating yourself up.

When you hold onto hurt, it permeates your soul and affects everyone and everything around you. To let go of the hurt, change your focus. Ask yourself, "What have I learned from the relationship?" It brought you something; maybe it brought you wonderful children; maybe it brought you insight you didn't have before. There will be something you gained, something that enriched your life. Therefore, have gratitude for the good and the perceived bad in your marriage. Be thankful, heal, and have closure. As you heal, you will feel your energy shift. As you heal, you will learn to live with yourself. You learn to love yourself. You learn that you truly are awesome!

Self esteem has often been shattered with disclosure. Remember, it was not your fault. It had nothing to do with your looks, your sexuality, or your personality. Tell yourself you are desirable, you are worthy of the life and relationship you desire. Reclaim your life. We are all responsible for our own lives and our own happiness. You are deserving of a compassionate, intimate relationship. You are deserving of being treated with respect. Relationships are meant to bring you joy.

"When we are no longer able to change a situation, we are challenged to change ourselves."

—Victor Frankl

Change and Transition

Change starts with new beginnings. Change is about shifting where we are or what we are doing. Transition is the process of dealing with the change. Transition is nothing less than the death and rebirth of your world. Honor the death of your world as it was; then look forward with joyful anticipation and intentions to your new world. You can do it; it just takes time. Do not expect too much too soon; visualize yourself and the future you want. Trust and have faith.

Determine where you are and where you want to be. What is your vision; what are your goals? Set priorities and plan your actions. Ensure that your actions are consistent with moving closer to where you want to be. You and you alone can make positive changes in your life. You are never too old for transition. You are never too old to go back to school, get a job, or experience a new love. What you see your life becoming is what it will become. Strive for happiness; get to that point where what you think, what you say, and what you do are in harmonious interaction. Take time to think; take time to reflect.

During transition, it is necessary to have support, which may come from a variety of places. It is best to look for groups that are aligned with your new way of thinking and that will encourage you to develop your ability to create your world. Intend to attract like-minded friends. Take classes that support your growth.

Letting go of the way things used to be can be very difficult. Sometimes we feel that by letting go we are saying that what happened did not matter—that the hurt our spouses caused us did not matter. Letting go, like forgiveness, is also for you. When your thoughts remain in the past, you bring those past vibrations into your present and future, creating more of the same. Creating more of the same does not bring us the happiness and love we strive for.

Often we are afraid to let go because letting go means releasing the old you. Sometimes it is easier to stay with what we know and to remain in our "comfort zone" no matter how detrimental it may be.

To let go of anything that is causing pain in your life, try the following exercise:

Write down on a piece of paper what it is you need to let go of. This can be something that has hurt you, a fear, or maybe a habit. When you have written down what you want to release, take the paper outside and in a safe place (fire pit, etc.) burn the paper and release these feelings to the universe. In this manner, you can release all that no longer serves you. Let go of the old, so you may embrace all the new coming into your life.

"God, grant me the serenity to accept the things I cannot change ... the courage to change the things I can ... and the wisdom to know the difference."

—Reinhold Niebuhr

"If you take each challenge one step at a time, with faith in every footstep, your strength and understanding will increase."

— James E. Faust

"Right now you are one choice away from a new beginning—one that leads you toward becoming the fullest human being you can be."

—Oprah Winfrey

Seeing Clearly

When I finally came to terms with the reality of our marital breakdown—when I knew I could no longer live in such a marriage—the lyrics to Johnny Nash's song, "I Can See Clearly Now," became my mantra.

I knew that there would be a rainbow after the rain. I knew that my life was about me. I could choose my direction. We all are able to choose our thoughts and choose our actions, and we can choose in accordance with our passion, with our core being. It takes courage to let go and to be true to ourselves and to focus our energy and thoughts on the direction we want our lives to take.

Too often, we equate the dissolution of a marriage with failure, and that fear of failure causes us to stay in relationships that no longer serve us. This can, quite literally, make us sick. To move forward, it is necessary to let go of the past, to let go of what we thought our lives were or were going to be, and to move forward to the lives we want to create.

Understand that you are worthy of love. Often, when we feel rejected in love, it causes limiting beliefs from our childhood to surface, making us think we are not worthy. You are worthy; you are lovable. Remember that limiting beliefs are thoughts that were placed in your subconscious mind by others. They are not facts. They are beliefs. You can change according to what you think, feel, and do.

Your husband may have hurt you by the things he said to you. Again, these are not who you are; they are what he said you were. You are worthy, you are smart; you are not a failure, you are not inadequate, and you are not any of the negative things you have been told. You are worthy of love, and you are worthy of the life you desire. Believe in yourself. Reclaim your power.

Again, it cannot be stressed enough, your thoughts are powerful. Your thoughts, feelings, and actions create your experiences. When you find yourself feeling worthless and unlovable, shift that thought to one that affirms your worthiness. Your feelings are not a result of what has happened; your feelings are a result of how you think about what has happened. So use your emotional guidance system, your intuition, to set the direction of your life. Learn how to consciously create your day, your life, living with intent.

"When you have a negative feeling, it is a sign that your thoughts are not taking you in the direction you want to go. Ask yourself throughout the day, 'How do I feel?' and if you discover you are feeling a negative emotion, you have the opportunity to change your thoughts ..."[9]

Remember to constantly read and speak your affirmations and your positive intentions. It takes approximately twenty-one days to change a habit. That is why repetition is necessary when you begin the process of living your life with intent. Say to yourself throughout the day:

"I am worthy."
"I expect and deserve the best."
"I love myself."
"I am lovable.

---

9   Elisabeth Fayt, *Paving It Forward* (New York: Morgan James Publishing, 2009), 12.

As you affirm, you are reprogramming your subconscious mind. Over time, through repetition, you will develop a new belief system, one of self-confidence and awareness. The more you affirm and expect the best, the better the circumstances and people you will attract into your life.

As you affirm, you will learn to live your life with intent, creating each moment of every day. This is simply a process of understanding that what you expect in life is what you get, so why not start expecting the best?

"I am open to receiving amazing gifts from the universe today ... surprise me!"

—Elisabeth Fayt

I live my life with gratitude.
Within me there is an abundance of love and joy.
I am lovable. I am loving.
I love myself.
I have released the pain of the past and live in the present.
I live each day with intent.
I surround myself with pleasant surroundings.
The people I attract into my life are loving, giving, and full of joy.
I am blessed, I am grateful.
Today is my day. This is my time.

—Carolyn M. Brown

"We must be willing to get rid of the life we've planned, so as to have the life that is waiting for us. The old skin has to be shed before the new one can come."

—Joseph Campbell

What is my new skin going to look like? We often hear that a middle-aged woman is not marketable in today's society. This is not true in the marketplace or in the dating world. You are what you believe you are. Empower yourself to be what you want to be. Create a new attitude, and remind yourself of this new attitude daily. Trust in yourself, trust your heart, and trust in God.

Trust that the hole you feel in your heart will be healed. The universe will always fill an empty space. Your life need not be lonely; you need not be alone. Take this as an opportunity to find out what you are passionate about and to follow your dreams.

You may not have any idea what it is you are passionate about, what really gets you excited, and what you would be doing if you felt there were no obstacles.

One way to live your life with intention is to get clear on what it is you want. This is a process. The first part of the process is to find your passion. The second part is to give yourself a "mind makeover."

Finding Your Passion

The key to discovering your passion, your destiny in life, is detailed in *The Passion Test* by Janet Bray Attwood and Chris Attwood.[10] It is a method they developed to help you determine your top five passions. Happy, successful people live their passions.

In the emotional upheaval and aftermath of discovering your husband is gay, you are not, as a rule, living your passion. Keep in mind that through this turmoil, you have discovered the need to "celebrate your life"—to live your life with intent, consciously creating your day, your life, and your experiences. It is time to discover what you are passionate about.

Once you discover your passions, you can develop your goals. When you have developed your goals, you can start to pre-pave™ and set your intentions; believe and be ready to receive.

So, "How do I find my passion?" you ask. Very simply: by following this two-step process.

Step One: Make a list of the top ten things you love, what you enjoy. If at first you are unsure of what it is you love, think about what makes you happy:

What do you enjoy doing?

---

10   Janet Bray Attwood and Chris Attwood, *The Passion Test* (New York: Hudson Street Press, 2007), 34.

What are you good at?

What is it you do that is so much fun you have no idea where all the time went?

What would you be doing if you felt there were no obstacles (money, time, etc.)?

What does your intuition tell you about what you want to do?

One way to develop your intuition is through meditation. It's just a matter of stopping long enough to listen to the divine within you; the answers are always provided.

I spent many hours in meditation after discovering the truth about my husband. Meditation is a very effective way to become in tune with yourself and the God within you. If you have difficulty meditating, start by spending some time in silence each day. Get quiet, be very present with yourself, and let the thoughts come and go. Eventually, you will start to generate answers.

At the time of my discovery, I was unaware of the "Passion test™." However, I was in the process of continuing my education as an adult. I knew it was important to me to finish my degree, not just for the financial opportunities, but because it was something I had always wanted in my life. I felt passionate about it.

I also knew I wanted to write a book, even though it took a few efforts to get my thoughts flowing in the right direction. I didn't want to write something negative or "tell my story"; I wanted to write something that would be empowering and uplifting.

I was passionate about developing a new relationship, about developing my spirituality. The one thing I did lack was vision and clarity. That is where the "Passion test™" and "Pre-paving™" made all the difference; they are perfect tools to rely on to provide vision, clarity, and the ability to expect that your life will unfold as you intend it

Step Two: Now that you have a list started the process is to then go through this list determining your top five passions. Compare the items, determining if you had to give up one, which one would it be? Continue this process until you are left with five items. These top five items provide clarity in determining your passion.

As Janet and Chris Attwood state, "When you are clear, what you want will show up in your life; and only to the extent that you are clear."[11]

I encourage you to visit the Passion test™ website (http://www. thepassiontest.com) and purchase the book in order to gain a more complete understanding of the passion test™ process.

I have also mentioned the technique of pre-paving™ several times and want to clarify exactly what that entails. The following excerpts from *Paving It Forward* by Elisabeth Fayt offer this explanation:[12]

A pre-pave™ is a statement of action or belief that you put forward to the Universe as a command. You mold your life by telling the Universe what you want.

Repetition is a big part of the learning process when you are shifting your consciousness to positive habits of thought. Certain habits of negative thought may have worked against you in the past. You need to lift the needle of your attention and shift it to a new spot, dropping it down onto a place that is line with manifesting what you want. At first the spot is slippery until it becomes a habit. This takes repetition.

Positive pre-paving™ is consciously choosing your thoughts and words for a specific result. When you set a pre-pave™ in motion, it physically "lines up the energy for its manifestation.

---

11 Janet Bray Attwood and Chris Attwood, *The Passion Test* (New York: Hudson Street Press, 2007), 40–42, 85.

12 Elisabeth Fayt, *Paving It Forward* (New York: Morgan James Publishing, 2009), 8, 12, 16.

What do you do when you have pre-pave™d something, but the Universe seemingly sends you something different? Sometimes past karma (the Law of Cause and Effect), or the result of past negative thoughts will bring into your current experience something that appears to go against what you want. If you acknowledge it as a manifestation of past thought and keep focused on your current positive pre-pave™ with sustained effort, you will create what you want.

Worry is a negative pre-pave™. The next time you have a negative thought, immediately turn it into its opposite, positive pre-pave™. Pave it forward with conviction. Feel it and mean it. The goal is to turn the positive pre-pave™ into a habit. This comes with daily practice in today mode. If you do enough today pre-pave™s, eventually, sooner than you think, you will be able to accomplish your goals as life-long habits. You must believe what you pave forward in order for it to work.[13]

I highly recommend Elisabeth's book as a guide to changing your life by pre-paving™. You may purchase it by visiting http://www.elisabethfayt.com.

At this point you might be wondering, "Okay, you have talked about passion and pre-paving™, but how do they work together?" My answer is, when you are clear about your passions, you can create them by pre-paving™. This means you become a deliberate creator in your life. What you think about, what you focus on, becomes your reality. When you are consciously creating your life every time you

---

13 Elisabeth Fayt, *Paving It Forward* (New York: Morgan James Publishing, 2009), 12.

are faced with a choice, ask yourself, "Is this decision in alignment with my passion? Is it in alignment with my higher purpose?"

The core of our essence is our soul. When our choices are not in alignment with our higher purpose, with our soul, we end up disappointed. Again, we create our lives by what we think, how we feel, and the actions we take. We alone are responsible for how we choose to act and how we choose to feel. When you consciously choose in favor of your passions, in favor of a higher purpose, you are telling the universe that you choose happiness. Happiness is what we really desire from life and what we really desire from love.

"When you are clear, what you want will show up in your life; and only to the extent that you are clear."

—Janet Bray Attwood and Chris Attwood

A Mind Makeover
Creating the Life You Really Want

CARE

CARE enough about yourself to:

Consciously

Aspire to

Reinforce and

Execute your passions ... and manifest what you want to create in your life.

Consciously ...

- You recognize that change needs to happen.
- You desire to create or transform your life (whatever you want to change).
- You have identified your limiting thoughts and beliefs and understand they are beliefs and not facts.
- You realize you are worthy of the life you desire.
- You have identified your passions. (Passions will change as you develop and achieve results ... revisit your passions every six months, or as your life manifests.)
- You set intentions and realize you are a deliberate creator of your life.

You know change needs to happen, but you are not sure what direction the change should take. Sometimes it takes a while to realize that only you can control the path of your life. The fact that your marriage is, or was not, what you thought is one thing. What you do with your life after this discovery is another. Determine the path you want for your life. The direction your life will take now is up to you. Be aware that you teach others how to treat you. Treat yourself with love and respect.

Identify your limiting thoughts and beliefs. We all have developed limiting thoughts and beliefs about ourselves. Again, these started in our childhood and are a result of things we have been told from family, friends, teachers, etc. These were never meant to have a lasting impact on us; however, we stored these messages in our subconscious and started to view them as facts. It is important to recognize that they never were facts. When you are conscious of your limiting beliefs, you can identify the thought patterns that need to change.

Identify and become conscious of what you want your new life to look like. Do you want marriage, a new career, to move, or to travel? What is your passion? How do you envision your life unfolding? What excites and moves you? What would you be doing with your life if anything was possible?

Identify the areas of your life where you want change. It might start with a change in your marriage as it is, or with divorce. You might want to change your health habits, you might want to move, or change careers. It is your life. You determine your destiny. Anything is possible.

Aspire ...

- To have a strong desire to make the change.
- To be willing to change your thoughts and behaviors.
- To become a creator of your life.
- To manifest your dreams.

It is necessary to have a strong desire to make the change happen. You cannot merely "wish" things were different. You cannot merely say, "What did I do to deserve this in my life?" Desire is stronger than a wish. The desire needs to be strong enough to recognize that achieving the result will mean there are things about you that need to be changed. It is only by changing our thoughts and our behaviors that we change our lives. As Einstein said, "Insanity is doing the same thing over and over and expecting different results."

When I was in the process of divorce and change, I had that quote, along with, "There is no try ... only do," posted on my bulletin board at work as a constant reminder of what I needed to do to change my life.

Reinforce ...

- Your awareness of your thoughts and feelings.
- Your ability to consciously shift negative thoughts to positive ones and reprogram your subconscious mind.
- Your use of positive affirmations every morning, every night, and throughout the day.

Be aware of your thoughts. When we have spent our lives living by default, it takes a concerted, conscious effort and reinforcement to learn how to live by intent. When you find yourself feeling sad or angry, ask yourself, "What is it I am thinking about?" When you are aware of the thought, you have the opportunity to change it.

Our thoughts do determine our lives. The more we focus on something that makes us angry, the stronger that emotion grows and the more we attract that negative aspect into our lives; thus, we remain stuck in our misery. When you become aware that your feelings impact the circumstances of your life, you will be able to shift your thoughts from negative to positive.

If you find yourself feeling angry, shift to a memory that makes you smile; call someone who will make you laugh; actively change your thoughts and feelings. Always be aware of your feelings and keep them on a high vibration, which will inevitably bring you closer to the life you envision.

Execute ...

- Your action plan.
- Your choices, aligning them with your passions and your higher self.
- Time spent in silence.
- The development and trust of your intuition.

> *See it* until you feel it.
> *Believe it* as though it has already happened.
> *Receive it* with gratitude and appreciation.

Live your life with intent. We often go through life living by default, letting the circumstances of life just happen. God gave us the power to have free will, to utilize this free will for the benefit of our lives. God gave us power; it is up to us to become synchronized with spirit, with our soul, in order to utilize this power for our well-being.

Again, I recommend meditating and spending time in silence. This will assist you in connecting to the spirit within you. It is through silence that we receive answers to our questions; it is how we develop our intuition.

Develop affirmations and conscious intentions to "reprogram" your subconscious. Your beliefs are formed by your subconscious. When you write and say affirmations, when you actively pre-pave™, your subconscious will take these as truths and your life will change. Examples include:

"I am a lovable person."
"I love my life."
"I love and appreciate myself."
"I am worthy of respect."

"I am a woman who deserves to be loved and cherished."

"I make wise choices."

"I radiate health and happiness."

"Everything I touch is a success."

Develop the affirmations that will work for you. Write these out on cards. Say them first thing in the morning and last thing at night. Look in the mirror and tell yourself how much you love yourself. It will feel strange at first, but over time you will come to believe it. Write out visionary note cards outlining your vision, your passion, as if it already existed.

"I am so happy, I am so grateful, now that I am …" Have these cards posted throughout your home; carry them with you and refer to these cards throughout the day.

Develop your action plan. What steps are you going to take to make change happen? Design a vision board. There are many ways to do this. You may do it on poster board; you may use your computer. You may have more than one vision board. Take action by:

- Establishing goals and priorities.
- Developing your approach, your action plan.
- Putting your plan into action.
- Setting a timeline for expected results (be realistic).
- Doing daily pre-pave^{TM}s
- Reviewing your progress—celebrate each small success. Revise as you manifest your desires.
- Visualizing your life as if you have already achieved your goals. Do this every day. It is up to you what direction your life takes. Expect change as a constant. Expect the best.

"Change is the natural law of life...I move from the old to the new with ease and joy."

—Louise Hay

"We must become the change we want to see."

— Mahatma Gandhi

Celebrate
Energy
Love
Embrace Life   You
Believe   Opportunities
Respect   Unique
Action
Thankful
Empower Yourself

Celebrate

To celebrate is to rejoice. Rejoice and celebrate the new life you are creating. Become a deliberate creator of your life.

Your thoughts, your actions, your feelings, and your emotions become your reality. You choose your thoughts. When you let go of the way you thought things were going to be, you open yourself to receiving the joys that are yours.

You are a person of courage. You have been faced with a challenge, and you have found the strength to overcome the challenge. You have learned that challenges make you grow, that challenges help you discover yourself and your passions.

Celebrate the passion in your life. Discover what excites you and what motivates you. Discover you.

Celebrate change. Change is a universal law. Change is a constant. Embrace change.

"Just as your car runs more smoothly and requires less energy to go faster and farther when the wheels are in perfect alignment, you perform better when your thoughts, feelings, emotions, goals, and values are in balance."

—Brian Tracy

Energy

Everything is energy. You are energy. Your thoughts are energy. You must focus on positive thoughts in order to emit positive vibrations. When you focus on negative thoughts, your vibrations are of a negative nature. You attract what you focus on, so choose to focus on positive, happy thoughts.

You might say, "How can I be happy? My marriage is in crisis."

The answer is, "Focus on what you want life to give you, focus on what was good about your marriage, and focus on the good in you."

Remember, you can control your thoughts; therefore, you control your feelings and emotions. The more your thoughts are about your unhappiness, the more unhappiness you will experience. When you feel unhappy, change that thought with something that makes you smile or laugh. This will change your energy vibration, and you will feel better and attract positive experiences.

"Love is life. And if you miss love, you miss life."

—Leo Buscaglia

Love

Love is powerful. Love has the highest vibrational frequency; therefore, love is the most powerful energy source. Remember, God is love! Love is meant to be joyous. Love is meant to enrich our lives, to enrich our spirit. We all seek love; however, with love, what we are seeking is happiness and acceptance.

We are all connected; our spirit and our souls are connected. We are one with spirit and one with each other. Appreciate that connection.

We all search for love; love should have laughter. Be with people who make you laugh and people who make you smile.

Above all, learn to love yourself. It is not selfish to love yourself. Others learn how to treat you by how you treat yourself. You can reprogram your mind by using affirmations and positive intentions. Tell yourself you love and approve of yourself, that you are worthy, and that you deserve happiness. Start each day with a pre-pave^{TM}. Intend for the best.

To receive love, give love.

"Health is the greatest gift, contentment the greatest wealth, faithfulness the best relationship."

—Buddha

"Do not dwell in the past; do not dream of the future. Concentrate the mind on the present moment."

—Buddha

Embrace Life

Embrace life. Embrace each day. Be grateful. Express appreciation for everything in your life. Wake up with a smile. Expect the best from each day. Tell yourself that you feel great.

Your health and your energy level are dependent upon your feelings. Those sad, unhappy days when you couldn't drag yourself out of bed and the tears made your eyes all swollen were days when your thoughts were focused on your pain. The only way to escape from that pain is to change your thoughts.

Recognize that each day is where you need to be. You decide how you are going to feel. Do not relinquish your power to others. Reclaim your power. Embrace the day.

Take time to exercise. When you exercise, you energize yourself. When you treat your body well, it spills over into your soul. When you treat yourself well, others will treat you well. Love your life!

"The greatest mistake you can make in life is to be continually afraid that you will make one."

—Ellen Hubbard

"Each difficult moment has the potential to open my eyes and open my heart."

—Myla Kabat-Zinn

Believe

When we believe, we regard things as being true; we have faith in what will happen. Believe in yourself. If you do not believe in you, no one else will. This is critical! *You must believe.* What you believe will become your reality. Believe that life is wonderful. Believe that you are capable of changing your life. Believe that your life is spectacular. Believe in God, the spirit, and the power within you.

Remember, what you ask for, what you believe in, you will receive. What is required is that you allow yourself to receive. Replace the doubt with belief.

Become who you want to be. Believe in miracles, and be thankful for each and every miracle, whether small or large.

"Respect starts with you."

—Proverb

Respect

Respect is showing esteem, giving honor. Respect yourself, and others will respect you. How we treat ourselves is how others learn to treat us. Be kind to yourself. Do not judge or criticize yourself. Do not say, "I should have done something different, I should have known, etc." You did nothing wrong; you made your choices based on what you knew at the time.

Be respectful in your communication with yourself and with others. Respect is about kindness, about caring, and about listening. You deserve respect. Others deserve respect. Each day, become the person you want to be.

"When you come to the edge of all the light you know, and are about to step off into the darkness of the unknown, faith is in knowing one of two things will happen: There will be something solid to stand on, or you will be taught how to fly."

—Barbara J. Winter

"Watch your thoughts, they become your words. Watch your words, they become your actions. Watch your actions, they become your habits. Watch your habits, they become your character. Watch your character, it becomes your destiny."

—Anonymous

Action

Action is the process of doing; it is the playing out of behaviors or habits. Take action in order to make change in your life. Actions must be in harmony with what we want our desired results to look like. Actions must be in alignment with our higher purpose and our passions in order to bring happiness.

It is impossible to achieve the vision of a great relationship if we are constantly thinking about how bad our relationships, or lack of relationships, happen to be. We cannot achieve peace and joy if our thoughts are constantly on anger and resentment. We must think and act as if our life is already joyous, as if our relationships are what we want them to be.

Act like you already have the life you dream of, and it will happen. The more passion you have for your life, the more you will be aligned to achieving the results you desire. Do not give up.

When you change to healthier eating habits, or you change your lifestyle and start to exercise, you experience a gap between your old body and your new body. This is also true when changing your life; there is a gap between the time you start living your life with intent and your manifestation.

Start with small intentions, such as light traffic, a wonderful day, or positively connecting with others. You will find things suddenly appearing, and you will realize there are no coincidences; you will realize you do bring about the events in your life. You will become excited about being in control.

Never give up. It is only by perseverance and by belief that the changes will appear.

"If you concentrate on finding whatever is good in every situation, you will discover that your life will suddenly be filled with gratitude, a feeling that nurtures the soul."

—Rabbi Harold Kushner

"Feeling grateful or appreciative of someone or something in your life actually attracts more of the things you appreciate and value into your life."

—Christiane Northrop

Thankfulness

What you are not thankful for, you take for granted. What you take for granted can disappear; and it is not until it is gone that you realize you miss it and should have been thankful.

Be sincere when giving thanks. It must come from the heart. Be thankful throughout the day. Begin and end each day with thanks.

Be thankful for the experiences of your marriage. When we look for the good, for the lessons in each experience, we will find that every experience brings us to a new and higher place.

Be thankful for family, for friends, for health, and for your home. Give thanks every morning, every night, and throughout the day.

Live your life with an *Attitude of Gratitude.*

"A happy person is not a person in a certain set of circumstances, but rather a person with a certain set of attitudes."

—Hugh Downs

Empowerment

You are responsible for you. Give yourself the power to change; give yourself permission to have the life and relationship you want, the one you know you deserve.

When you remain angry and bitter, you give your power away. By forgiving yourself and forgiving others, you let go and thereby regain your power.

Your choices, your thoughts, and your actions are what create your life.

You do not have to settle. Nowhere is it said that you are selfish if you do not want to settle. When you hold true to your convictions, your values, and your dreams, you are secure and confident. With confidence comes empowerment. Take control of your life. Live each day with intent, with purpose, and with gratitude.

"It takes courage to grow up and become who you really are."

—e.e. cummings

"I dream my painting, and then I paint my dream."

—Vincent Van Gogh

You

Regardless of how you move on, you will always, at one time, have been married to someone gay. Your children will always have a gay father. This is okay. It is part of your life. It will always be a part of your life; it is what brought you to where you are today and is what is helping you to decide where you are going. You learned from it, and you will grow from it.

You might be thinking, *I don't know what I want my life to look like. I don't know what I want from life.*

The answer is to start with what you don't want. You are aware of what you don't want. Take a sheet of paper and draw a line down the middle. On one side, list what you don't want; on the other side, list its opposite. For example, "I don't want a husband who is gay" changes to, "I want a husband who is heterosexual, whose sexuality and desires are compatible with mine."

"I don't want to be in debt" changes to, "I want financial freedom."

Then take the "I want" side and rework it to a list of what is most important to you. Write these out on your note cards to refer to every day. Tear up the "what you don't want list" and *never, ever* again refer to what you don't want. Remember, those words are eliminated from your vocabulary. Focus on the life you do want. Keep your energy vibration at a high level. What you focus on is what you attract.

Change your thoughts, change your actions; *you will see it when you believe it.*

"When one door closes, another opens, but we often look so regretfully upon the closed door that we don't see the one that has opened for us."

—Helen Keller

Opportunities

An opportunity is a chance for progress. Life is full of opportunity. We choose how we view our life experiences. We choose to advance or retreat from the circumstances of life.

Life is full of lessons. Take life's challenges and turn them into opportunities. View the blessings in all of life's circumstances. No matter how bad we feel about the things that have happened to us, there is always something to be found in that experience to be grateful for. Be open to new ideas. Your world is opening up before you! Give thanks for the opportunity to grow! Everything is an opportunity for growth. Embrace the opportunity; embrace life.

"Every time you don't follow your inner guidance, you feel a loss of energy, loss of power, a sense of spiritual deadness."

—Shakti Gawain

Unique

You are one of a kind. You are unique. You are special. Your circumstances might not be unique, but how you choose to handle them is. The responsibility is ultimately yours.

Do not see yourself as a victim, as someone who is powerless. Trust and have faith in you. You are unique; you have special talents, passions, and dreams. Be proud of your accomplishments, your courage, and your strength.

Affirm your acceptance and love for yourself daily. Live in the present; vision your future. Be excited about life; be enthusiastic. Remember what it is like to be a child with all the possibilities of life before you.

Be open to the universe and all its magnificence. Let your life unfold as it should.

Moving On

The following excerpt from Iyanla Vanzant's book, *Until Today*, the devotion for May 16, states we need to know how to cover the hole in our hearts in order to move on:

I am now receptive to the idea that ... whenever **I see a hole, I am to move around it.** Somebody left you, and now there is a gaping hole in the middle of your soul. The question is how are you going to fill that hole? Are you going to fill it with the painful memories of how you got hurt or got left? Or are you going to fill it with memories of the many moments of joy and laughter you had together? Are you going to fill the hole with anger, resentment, fear, or shame directed toward the one who left? Or are you going to fill the hole with appreciation that you do have an opportunity to choose how you are going to fill the hole. Are you going to fill the hole with the countless reasons why it should not have happened to you? Or are you going to fill it with the courage it will take to accept that it did happen to you in this way? Are you going to fill the hole with at least one ounce of confidence that you can handle this, whatever it takes? Or are you going to fill the hole with the self-defeating belief that you can't or will not make it through or over this hole? Are you going to empty all of your self-value, self-worth, and self-esteem into the hole until it becomes a pit of self-pity, self-doubt, and self-inflicted nonsense that keeps you in a hole of despair? Are you going to throw yourself into a hole and dare life to try and move you?

You can cover the hole with love and prayer and acceptance of your ability to step over or walk around the hole. You can also step back, take a little break, and wait to see the Self that emerges from the hole. The choice is yours.

Until today, you may have believed that you had to stay in the painful hole of hurt caused by the loss of a loved one. Just for today make a conscious effort and choice to cover the hole and move on.

Today I am devoted to covering the holes and filling in all the gaps in my life."[14]

---

14   Iyanla Vanzant, *Until Today* (New York: Simon and Schuster, 2001).

"God is Love; his plan for creation can be rooted only in love. Does not that simple thought, rather than erudite reasonings, offer solace to the human heart? Every saint who has penetrated to the core of Reality has testified that a divine universal plan exists and that it is beautiful and full of joy."

— Paramahansa Yogananda

Is there joy in your life? Are the day-to-day interactions in your relationship meeting your needs, or are you faced with constant mistrust and renegotiation? Do not sacrifice yourself. If you are not happy, all of your relationships and interactions will suffer. Recognize it is essential to focus on your well-being. If you are not in a state of well-being, you cannot function. Focusing on you is not selfish.

Other than God, your first and primary relationship is with yourself. The relationship you have with you reflects your relationships with others. You need to love and appreciate yourself, to work on healing yourself.

Do not relinquish your heart. It is possible to find love and joy in a relationship without it seeming like work. We are told to pick careers we enjoy; when we do what we find satisfying, it will not seem like work. This is also true in marriage; when your relationship is filled with joy, laughter, intimacy, and a shared faith, the marriage does not seem like work.

Work is effort, and living with the one you love should not be an effort; it should be joyful and full of laughter. When you have joy and laughter, you are able to discern what is important and what isn't. When you can do this, it is possible to communicate in ways that are not hurtful to your relationship.

Remember, once you know the truth, you cannot go back to not knowing. It is all about you, what you are going to do with your new knowledge, how you are going to heal, and how you are going to grow. This is your life. Find the passion in your life, purposely intend, and become a creator of your life. Celebrate your life.

You ... Celebrate You!

You ... Celebrate You!
Carolyn M. Brown

www.amindmakeover.com
www.youcelebrateyou.com
youcelebrateyou@gmail.com

For speaking engagements, seminars, or interviews, e-mail or refer to the website for additional information.

References

Elisabeth Fayt, *Paving It Forward* (New York: Morgan James Publishing, 2009).

Iyanla Vanzant, *Until Today* (New York: Simon and Schuster, 2000).

Janet Bray Attwood and Christ Attwood, *The Passion Test* (New York: Hudson Street Press, 2007).

Online References

http://marriage.about.com/cs/straightspouses/a/straightspouse.htm last accessed, November 7, 2010.

http://education.yahoo.com/reference/dictionary/entry/shame, last accessed, November 7, 2010.

http://ancienthistory.about.com/cs/grecoromanmyth1/g/phoenixbird.htm, last accessed November 7, 2010.

http://straightspouse.org/home.php.

http://marriedgay.org, accessed, November 7, 2010.

Suggested Resources

Dr. Wayne W. Dyer, *Change Your Thoughts—Change Your Life* (New York: Hay House, Inc., 2007).

Dr. Wayne W. Dyer, *Manifest Your Destiny* (New York: Harper Collins, 1997).

Deepak Chopra, *The Seven Spiritual Laws of Success* (San Rafael, CA: Amber-Allen Publishing, 1993).

Endorsements

"You are about to embark on an authentic journey. Carolyn's book covers it all: humanity, love, compassion, forgiveness, joy, and celebration. Her fresh approach is deeply moving. The book provides real tools to move you forward in your life. You will remember these life teachings for years to come."
Shawne Duperon
Media and Gossip Expert
Five-time EMMY® Award Winner
www.shawnetv.com

"This book is a must read for anyone who has an awakening and is asking him or herself, 'Who is this person I married?'"
Daniel Gutierrez
Best-selling Author, International Speaker, Trainer, and Radio Personality
www.danielgutierrez.com

"I believe that Carolyn will be the candle that others will light their candles from. Get ready to have your heart and mind opened; I trust you will."
Elisabeth Fayt, International Speaker
Author of *Paving It Forward*
www.pavingitforward.com

www.ingramcontent.com/pod-product-compliance
Lightning Source LLC
Chambersburg PA
CBHW020435290526
45785CB00002B/858